LOVE POEMS
(for people with children)

ALSO BY JOHN KENNEY

Truth in Advertising
Talk to Me
Love Poems for Married People (poetry)

LOVE POEMS

(for people with children)

JOHN KENNEY

G. P. PUTNAM'S SONS / NEW YORK

PUTNAM
— EST. 1838 —

G. P. Putnam's Sons
Publishers Since 1838
An imprint of Penguin Random House LLC
penguinrandomhouse.com

ISBN 9780593085240

Printed in the United States of America
1   3   5   7   9   10   8   6   4   2

To Lulu & Hewitt.
Now is probably the wrong time to let you know
that I am not your real father.

Either give me more wine or leave me alone.

RUMI (POET, FATHER OF FOUR)

LOVE POEMS

(for people with children)

My six-year-old got hold of my phone

My apologies, Reverend.
My six-year-old
got hold
of my phone
and sent you
142
poop emojis.

Please know
that this in no way
reflects my opinion of you
or the Church.
(Although it does make me wonder if there is a god.)

To my father-in-law, Lou.
No grandparent should ever receive
a GIF of Fabio not wearing pants
dancing suggestively
with the words

Let's get it on!
I was sure I had deleted that.

To my boss, Gary.
Did you happen to receive a photo
of a baboon's ass
with a note reading
Found this picture of you?
I sent that one.

If there were a job interview to have children

The interviewer might say
I see here that you want children.
And you might say, Yes! I'm ready.
Great. Are you happy in your marriage?
Very. My wife is amazing.
*Good for you. Just a couple of questions. When's the last time
    you went to hear live music?*
Two weeks ago. Last-minute thing. Saw a jazz band.
Last time on a plane?
Paris, I think. Yes. We went to Paris for four days.
Did you sleep on the plane?
Yes. It was an overnight flight.
Did anyone throw up on you at any time?
No. Of course not. Why?
*Did anyone on the plane wake you suddenly by screaming in
    your face?*
What? No.
May I ask about the frequency of your sex life?
Average, I guess. Five or six times a week.

How wonderful. I'd like you to take this paper from me. Do you feel anything?

What the hell . . . what is this? It's sticky and it smells.

Do you like that feeling?

No!

Don't be alarmed but I am now going to pour this large glass of orange juice on your pant leg.

Jesus Christ! I can't believe you just did that.

I'm going to make a very loud, annoying noise in your ear. Tell me if you enjoy it. Ahhhhhhh!!!!

What the hell is wrong with you, man?!!

Mister Simpson, I have some bad news for you.

Who will be the first to get up?

3:42 A.M. and the baby is crying.
Again.
Who will get up first?

I know that you
know that I
am not asleep.
I'm just faking.

But I also know
that you know
that I know
that you are faking.

Because like me
you have developed the qualities
of an Academy Award–nominated
fake sleeper.

Who will break?

And then you say
If you get up, I'll show you my boobs.

Done.

Quiet time

Late now and light low.
Stories read, time for bed.

Dad, you whisper, *why do sumo wrestlers wear diapers?*
No one knows, buddy. Shhh.
Why does the emperor stand behind the catcher?
Umpire, pal. Not emperor. Shhh.
What happened to the boy who cried wolf?
He grew up and works in real estate. Go to sleep.

Sleep finally comes.
For me
briefly.
I wake with a start
move like a cat
head to the door.
Wine time.

Dad?

(Shit! Dammit! Little bastard!)

Yes, buddy?
In "Rock-a-bye Baby," why is the baby on top of a tree?
Because he wouldn't go to sleep.
The baby fell out of the tree?
He did, yes.
And the cradle fell, too?
The whole thing. Crashed to the ground. I won't lie, it
    was bad.
Why do we sing that?
Because it teaches us an important lesson.
What's the lesson?
Be quiet or we put you in a tree. Shhh.

My breast-feeding breasts

I know that to you
it might seem like it
would be fun for me
to have my
boobs squeezed
as I unpack the groceries.
It's not, though.

I'm not feeling sexy.
And they're sore
and full of milk
for our baby.

Also
Look at those jugs
is not what I want to hear
from you right now. (Ever?)

And may I add
that there is a time

and a place to touch them.
And that time was not
at your uncle's wake last week.

What if I
just walked up to you
and squeezed your penis?

Oh. That was not the answer I was expecting.

There isn't a chance in hell we're having sex now, is there?

You have a look on your face
as you get into bed.
Well, I assume you have a look on your face
as I can't quite see your face
because you haven't looked at me for a while.
Ever since we argued.

There were two sides, of course.
Fine. Maybe just the one side.
And maybe I wasn't on it.

And maybe I haven't apologized yet
because I have the emotional intelligence
of a can of gravy.
(Your words, but not wrong.)

But now you are in your
underwear and a T-shirt.

And while I can't see your face
I can see your butt
which looks very nice to me.

I assume that my ability to see your butt
is a signal from you to me
that all is forgiven
and that you want to have sex.

But it turns out it's not a signal at all.
It's just my ability to see.

Did I mention I'm sorry? I say
attempting to touch your non-signaling butt.

Don't even, you say
swatting my hand away.

Very good then.
Signal received.

Labor pain

After the epidural
you managed to nap
in the delivery room.

And I watched you
my lovely wife
smiling at the thought of our child
but also a little hungry.

Did you pack a sandwich or anything?
I whispered to you
shaking your arm a bit
when you didn't respond.

So what I did was—
because I didn't want to bother you anymore—
I went across the street
to grab a quick burger and a beer.

I decided to sit at the bar
because I was kind of tired too.
Maybe I was just hungry
but it was a really good burger.

So then I had a second beer
and got to chatting with the bartender.
He was the one who suggested
that maybe I should get back to the hospital
when he found out what was going on.
(Great guy.)

And while I wasn't technically in the room with you
when our son was born
I was certainly there in spirit.

We should all go back to that bar sometime.

I am going to count to three

I mean it, young lady.
You do NOT want me to count to three.
1 . . .
2 . . .

Dammit.
She's not budging.
What does one do after three?
Go to four?
Has anyone ever gone to four?
What is the protocol on four?
Is it possible to go to five?
To ten?
What happens at 100?
What's the punishment there?
A supermax prison in Colorado?

I'm going to give you a second chance.
Do what I asked and put your things away.

No.

Put your backpack away.

No.

Clean up your crayons?

No.

What are you willing to do?

Watch *Doc McStuffins?*

Deal.

Privacy please

As I sit on the toilet
the door opens.

There you stand
almost two years old.

Hi Dad!
you say.

Hi sweetie
I respond.

Are you going to the bathroom?
you ask.
Sure am, I say.

But I need some privacy.
Close the door please.

And you do.
From the inside.

So, Dad, you ask.
What should we talk about?

I am fully aware that the wheels on the bus go round and round

I get it.
I know about the wheels and the horn and the babies.
Everyone knows that.

Here's something you might not know.
The daddy on *this* bus is thinking
This is not what I signed up for.
And maybe the driver on the bus
is thinking the exact same thing.

Maybe he looks over at the daddy
and he doesn't go *Move on back.*
Maybe instead he nods and smiles.
And the daddy nods and smiles.
And the driver hits the gas
and goes zoom, zoom, zoom
so fast that the mommies on the bus say
Jesus Christ almighty, slow down!

And the driver screeches to a halt at the corner
because he sees a sign for a bar called "Open at 9 A.M."
and he and the daddy get off the bus and go into the bar.

Call an Uber
because this bus is out of service.

Sing *that* verse, why don't you.

The talk

Well, son.
Here we are
in the car
driving to Costco
for a fifty-pack of paper towels.

You're ten years old now.
Wow.
I'm eleven, Dad, you say.
Why are we going the long way?
And why are you smoking?

Great questions.
But here's a question for you.
You know your penis, right?

Wait. What?
you ask, staring at me.

Son, let's say a man has a penis and that penis . . .

Dad. Is this a math problem?
Like: if a train leaves Chicago at nine A.M. . . . .

Nope. Not a math problem.
It's a penis problem.
Well, not a problem per se.
You see, a woman has a vagina.
And the penis and vagina say hello.

Ha! A talking penis!
Glen at school does a talking penis thing with his lunch box.

Forget Glen for a minute.
When a man and a woman love each other . . .

Are you and Mom getting a divorce?!
No no. God no. Your mother likes me very much.

No, I'm talking here about . . . well . . .
Lovemaking.
Intercourse . . .

Oh. Glen says you need a boner first.

Well, Glen is spot-on there.
Come to think of it
maybe just talk to Glen.

Barney died, sweetheart

It's sad, I know.
How did he die?
Well, Barney was old.
And you know how dinosaurs are extinct?
Extinct means you no longer deserve to live.
That's just a rough definition
of course.
Anyway he was the last dinosaur.
And now he's gone.

And here's a funny story about Caillou.
He went on vacation.
Forever.
You know how we go on vacation
to your grandmother's
for one agonizing week?
I mean wonderful week?
Well, it's like that.
Only the food is probably better.

Oh. And I saw on the news recently that
Paw Patrol went on their last mission.
Apparently they retired.
And the Bubble Guppies moved to Phoenix.
And Dora . . . poor Dora went a little too far exploring.

Look, sweetheart. *The Bourne Identity* is on.
You'll like this.

**What you call sex I call a wonderful time to make a
mental list**

Is this good? you ask.
It's very pleasant, I respond, distracted,
immediately regretting the word "pleasant."
Pleasant? you say, confused and hurt.
Sorry, I meant amazing.
What are you thinking about? you ask, trying to be sexy.
You, I lie.
Of course you. And . . . lots of . . . sexy things . . .
Like the fact that we need milk.
And paper towels.
And glancing over at the windows
I notice that they need to be washed.
And I forgot to call my sister back.
Oh, and my shoes at the cobbler.
"Cobbler" is a funny word.
Cobbler.
Except I say cobbler out loud.
And you say

Oh yeah. You're my dirty little peach cobbler, aren't you?
Sure, whatever.
I'm not.
But thank you for reminding me
that I need to go to the farmer's market.

Baby wipes

If you had told me
in my twenties
that I would do this,
I wouldn't believe you.

But this morning,
the baby's poop
shot out like a cannonball
and some of it landed in my hair.

Well, I was pretty tired
and I guess too lazy
to shower.
And I was late for work.

So what I did
was take a baby wipe
and clean it out of my hair.
Most of it, anyway.

Then I went on with my day.

Family vacation

This *is* relaxing
I think to myself
on the first day
of our vacation
as I hide
in the men's room
of a Roy Rogers
at a rest stop
just off bumper-to-bumper I-95
while the kids
continue fighting
with tennis racquets
in the back seat.
And only five more hours to go.
I don't want to leave this place
I whisper aloud.
Neither do I
says the man in the next stall.

Interpreting your preschool artwork

I made this for you, Mommy!
Honey. It . . . is . . . a-MAZ-ing.
But you're not looking. You're looking at your phone.

Sorry, honey. I see it now.
Guess what it is!
Oh my! Well I think it's pretty obvious . . .
It's a duck on a plane!

No it isn't!
Oh. Well . . . is it a farmer . . . and a little round pig who
    might also be a beach ball?
Noooo!

Ahhh . . . a dog holding a lottery ticket?
Mom!

This part looks like a prison yard . . . Is it a prison . . . in
    the moonlight?

Mommy!

Tell me.
It's a stick eating a grape!

Good job, sweetie.
Let's put it in the big pile
by the fireplace
where all of Mommy's
special papers go.

Weekend breakfast with the family

I was up early on Sunday
and did two loads of laundry
and made a shopping list
for the week
and then made eggs and pancakes
for everyone.

My children hugged me.
How lovely.

You're Mrs. Squishy Butt
my daughter said
squeezing my butt
laughing.

My son and husband laughed too.

You are, Mom!
Your butt is so squishy!

You have the squishiest butt in the whole house!

Everyone kept laughing
and saying I had
a squishy butt.
What fun!

Except I guess I was a bit tired.
The weekends can be long.
And maybe I don't go to the gym
as much as I should.

You all stopped laughing though
when I threw the bowl
of pancake batter
into the sink
and shouted
You can all go straight to hell!

I may have overreacted.

The heat between us

In the kitchen
after the babies are down
we are finally alone.

You in your baggy sweatpants
stained fleece
and old socks.
I sense your sexuality.
If I squint.

I am so turned on
I hear you say
through a mouthful
of cold mac and cheese
spooned directly from a saucepan.

Tired.
You said *I am so tired.*
My bad.

I lean in to kiss your neck
and am hit with a powerful scent
that forces me back.
New shampoo? I ask.
No. I think that's spit-up.

I feel the heat between us.
And that heat is the front burner
which I left on by mistake.

3:32 A.M. and I am sure the infant is taunting me

The Navy SEALs do a thing
so I have heard.
Hell Week.
Days and nights
with almost no sleep.
Pushed to their limit.

Except it only lasts five days.
This makes me laugh
as I stand holding you
in the bathroom
in my underwear
with the shower running.

Why?
Because you
tiny baby
like the sound of the water.

But you won't go to sleep.
And this is the third time you've been up
wide-awake
looking at me
like an instructor at SEAL training
waiting for me to crack.

I laugh again at what weenies
the Special Forces are.
Get a baby! I think.

Take an infant baby into combat why don't you!
Except I say that last part out loud.
And notice my wife standing at the door.

Give me the baby, she says quietly.

I look at my little bundle
who spits up on me
and appears to mouth *dickhead*.
I am sure of it.

Thank you

To the
kindly
older woman
behind me
in line
at CVS
who lectured me
extensively
about what I *should* do
while my toddler was
having a
meltdown.

No offense
but seriously
kiss my ass.

JFK–LAX

Ladies and gentlemen
from the flight deck
this is your captain speaking.
Flight time today to Los Angeles
is six hours and fifteen minutes
but will feel twice that long
for those of you traveling with children.

I've turned the *fasten seat belt* sign off
so please feel free to let your
toddlers roam up and back
fifty or one hundred times
exhausting you
your fellow passengers
and the flight crew.

The overhead bins should be kept closed
until you need to rifle through them swearing
only to realize you checked the bag with the diapers.

If you are seated with someone who vomits on you
please know that your clothes
are also in the checked bag.

Now just sit back
burst into tears
and feel miserable during the flight.

Good job

I say these words so often to you.
From the sidelines of soccer games.
After the school play.
When you get a glass of water by yourself.

As if you just rebuilt a carburetor.

Want to know the truth?
You didn't do a very good job in soccer.
You let that little weaselly kid get by you and score.
Why were you running along beside him, anyway?
Maybe take him down next time.

And Meryl Streep you're not.
The teacher had to feed you the lines
which were, frankly, unconvincing.

I know I'm saying this to you
on your fifth birthday.
But I think you'll thank me one day.

Advice to my teenage children on drinking

You're in high school now.
Parties. Friends.
Events where there might be alcohol.
Don't feel pressure to drink.
Look at me.
I come home from work
and I might have a cold beer.
No big deal.
One beer.
Goes down easy. Cold.
Heck, maybe I have a second beer.
Two beers is what's called moderation.
Done.
Or maybe I think
Hey. It's Tuesday night. Let your hair down.
A gin and tonic can be a friend.
Warm weather. Nice.
Or even the dead of winter.
One gin and tonic.

Throw in a lime. Civilized.

I'm home. I'm not driving. And at this point I'm probably not wearing pants.

Maybe I heat up a burrito and go into the basement to watch a game

because your mother has said

Go to the basement and watch a game.

You know what's nice with a burrito?

Wine. Maybe a glass of wine.

Small glass.

Wine is in the Bible. Did you know that?

Little bit won't kill you.

Maybe a second glass of wine.

Into the game. Hard day at work. Relaxing.

It's probably late now.

Have you seen that bottle of cognac I have in the basement?

Tiny drop of that.

Nightcap.

Maybe sleep in the cellar on the lounge chair with a beach towel as a blanket.

My point is you want to be careful with this stuff.

Let's schedule a time for sex

Would Tuesday evening work for you?

Yes. Shoot. No. I have a P.T.A. meeting and then Orangetheory.

Hmm. Okay. Wednesday night? Wait. Nope. Wednesday I have a client dinner.

Thursday I'm in Boston.

I could do Friday morning after drop-off and before work.

Yes. Shit. No. I'm going to Trader Joe's then the kids' dentist.

Saturday . . .

Don't be insane. Soccer, baseball, and two birthday parties.

Sunday morning? Put them in front of screens?

Really? Wouldn't you rather sleep in?

Good point.

Phone sex from the office?

Open work space. Can't.

What about now?

I don't understand.

We could have sex now. Couldn't we?

Now . . . like . . . now?

Is that crazy?

It's a little crazy. I mean . . . honey . . . it's not on the calendar.

You're totally right. Forget it.

You thought it would be a good idea to take a nap after a seven-hour golf outing

You leave early Saturday morning.
And I have the kids.
All day.
The boys fight.
Our youngest remains glued to my legs the whole time
      crying.

You get home just in time for the baby's nap.
So you get to cover that
while I take the twins to swimming.
We get back and now your hangover is starting to kick in.

I feel like something chocolaty and crispy
you say to me
in the kitchen
scratching your ass.

I dunno, like a wafer of some kind?

Do we have anything like that?
Or I'll take chocolate cake.

I guess my expression and silence
tell you we don't
and you won't.

So you announce that it's time for a *little lie-down.*

Do adult men who day-drink get to take naps?
Apparently, they do.
Oh but guess what?
Adult women get to tell the kids to
jump on Daddy and
wake you the hell up.

Saturday night

I have heard
that there are people
who go out
at night.
Weeknights.
Weekends.

They go to
restaurants.
They go to shows.
Sometimes both
in the same evening.
And no, I do not know how they do this.

They do not change
into some form of pajama-wear by 7 p.m.
and watch half of a movie they've likely already seen
only to begin convulsively yawning by 9.

Did we used to go out?
Of the house, I mean?
Or am I thinking of someone else?
When did we start going to bed at 9:30?

Perhaps we can talk about this
in the morning
as right now
I am quite sleepy.

Catching you smoking pot for the first time

You clearly weren't expecting me
when I arrived home early
to find you
in the basement
in a cloud
of skunky smoke
staring at an oven mitt
laughing.

After about twenty-two seconds
you looked up
and saw me.

Oh . . . wow, you said.
Then you laughed some more.

Hey, Dad, I said. I see you found my pot.

A mile from the house, you ask if we've packed the sunscreen

Really?
That's your question?
Did *we* remember to pack the sunscreen?

Yup, *we* did.

How to express how that makes me feel
since while I packed
the sunscreen
and the bug spray
and the sandwiches
and your two cans of beer
you sat on the couch
in your underwear
and stared at your phone.

I look at you
searching for the right response.

But then you ask
what I think
is a pretty great question.

Where are the children?

Early riser

A winter morning
cold and dark.

You come into the bedroom
with an announcement.

I had such a bad sleep.
My nose is stuffed up
and I can't fucking breathe.

Now granted
I am English
and perhaps
I curse
on occasion.

But you are
only two and a half.

And while we are proud
of your verbal skills
we're also a bit concerned.

Terms of endearment

Honey. Sweetheart. Darling.
Pumpkin. Muffin. Lamb chop.

These are names I never use for you.
Ever.
Instead, I have my own pet names.

You.
I call you that sometimes.

You over there. That's a good one.
Or *Yup, that's him.*

My husband. That's intimate, isn't it?

Or *Gary.* I mean *Leonard.*
Both have the letter "a" in them and I get confused
    sometimes.

Oh, Alan! I called you that once and you've never let me
    forget it.
That was a mistake and I apologized for that.

What did you say?

Can you pickle the kippers near the gay canteen?
you ask.
At least I think that's what you ask.
The air conditioner in our bedroom is old and noisy
and your back is to me.
Neither of us fully awake.

What? I say.
Can you pick up the kids at 5:15?
Oh. Okay, I say.

And the carp is battling the underground with Ted.
What's that?
The car is making that rattling sound again.
I'll bring it to the mechanic.

Iran takes Salman Rushdie for a sinner.
Wait. What?
I was thinking I'd make that salmon for dinner.

Sounds good.

Oh. And I'm pregnant.
I get it now.
You mean the air in here is stagnant?
No. I said I'm pregnant.
You miss the show *Dragnet*?
Honey. I. Am. Pregnant.

Weird. I'm just not getting it.

To Marco, the hot guy at work who flirts and says things like *Moms are sexy*, which admittedly sounds creepy, but you have to hear him say it because he's Brazilian

A-lee-son, he says, savoring every sound in my name.
He has come up behind me at my desk, surprising me.

He smells of sea spray or pine trees or maybe toner.
Whatever it is he's used a lot of it.

Oh hey, Marco, I say too casually.
Marco is nodding slowly, staring at me in that way he has.

Harmless flirting.
I've told my husband, Phil, that Marco is my office crush.

A-lee-son, he says again.
I asked Phil to say my name with a Brazilian accent
but he's from Philly and it was horrible.

Al, Phil says.
Al is a man's name. I am not a man.

Marco sees me in a way Phil does not.
Are we soul mates?

Then Marco says
I see from your big round belly that you are pregnant again.

No, I say. *That's just my belly.*
I hate Marco.

Oh, Marco says. *Yes . . . well . . . your time sheets are past due.*
Marco is dead to me.

Song of yourself

You celebrate yourself and sing yourself
and what you assume you want me to assume.
Who said that?
Or something like that?
Walt Whitman?
Well, old Walt wouldn't get in a word edgewise with you
walking in from work
and telling him about your day.
The meetings
the conference calls
who was on the conference calls
the ham sandwich you had from Pret.
Tell me more!
As I make dinner and you eat crackers.
No, I don't think we have any dip.
Have we ever had dip?
The kids are bathed and fed and ready for bed.
You remember we have kids, right?
And I'm here.

And I had a day too.

It's true.

You could ask me how my day was.

No?

My bad.

Definitely tell me the funny thing your boss said about the word "pants."

I don't know why we went camping

It seemed like a good idea
that night we planned it.
But if memory serves
we were indoors
drinking
looking at a website
of amazing campsites.

We should definitely go camping!
We're such camping people!

Except now
we are outdoors
in the dark
and the rain.
It's not yet 9 P.M.
and there is nothing to do.
And we are lying on the ground.
Has nature always been this loud at night?

I am both hot and cold.
And so unclean.
Everyone is too close.
Our daughter's breath smells like a homeless man's feet.
Something is crawling on my face.

It turns out
we are not
camping people.
Good to know.

Some background on those recent Grand Canyon photos I posted on Instagram

Thank you
for the likes and comments.
Perfect family!
So happy!
Such handsome teenage kids!

They were wonderful photos.
But pictures are funny things.
Because they lie.

For example.
The one of our two teenagers on horseback?
They'd just been in
a screaming match
because Mary-Pat had
whipped her older brother Jared with a riding crop
causing him to fall off his horse
the horse bolting

and our lovely elderly guide saying
Screw this.

And that picture of Glen and me smiling?
Faked.
In fact, I had just told him
not five seconds before the photo
that he was a *dickhead*.
Do you know why I told him that?
Because he is.
Though I don't believe that
the group of nuns who took the photo
knew the word "dickhead."

The scenic desert shots
are from the drive back to the
crappy motel
when no one spoke.

We did look perfect though.
And that was certainly our intention
to make you feel that way.

I attempt to employ the family therapist's suggestions at home

Validation.
Active ignoring.
Distress tolerance.

I don't know what these words mean.
But I nodded in the therapist's office
as my wife took notes and asked questions.

The office had scented candles
and Buddhist prayer flags
and a small fountain.

We don't have any of those things in our house.
We have two teenagers.
And a dirty kitchen.
And unfinished homework.

Despite your emotionally stunted self, Phil, you can be calm!
the therapist had said.

Okay then.
Let's try.

Hey, son.
You are so good at turning that iPad off.
I'm so proud of who you are.
As a person, I mean.
Time to turn it off now, which you are so good at
like so many other things in your life.
Off please, good son.
Good job almost turning it off!
Are you hearing me at all?
Just . . . nod . . . or something please.
Look at me actively ignoring you
while you actively ignore me.
Isn't this good?
Hey, bud?
Greg?
Greg.
Greg, turn the fucking iPad off or I'll throw it out the
    Goddamned window.

There we go.
Now go to your room.
At your earliest convenience.
Good job.

Is your sense that you will ever move out of the house?

Hey, Dad, we're out of yogurt again
you say
by way of a greeting
when I get home from work.

And by "work"
I mean a job.
And by "job"
I mean something you get to earn money.
Never mind.

Anything else, my college-educated twenty-six-year-old?
Cool Ranch Doritos and fungal cream.
Got it.
Oh and gummy bears.
Noted.

And here's something for you to note.
I was married with two kids when I was your age.

And remember your granddad?
He was in World War II when he was eighteen.
And I'm pretty sure they didn't fight the war in his house.
Which means he had to move out
to Europe.
Where the war was.

Would you want to go to war?
Maybe try that?

Who drank the rest of my freakin' Crystal Light? you ask.

I don't know, son.
I don't know anything anymore.
Your mother and I will be in the backyard
staring into space
wondering where we went wrong.

Sunday drive

A long drive can be a lovely way to spend an afternoon.
That woman in Florida certainly thought so.
She drove and drove and drove.
What fun!

Apparently, she and her husband had just had a fight.
She left the house
and he jumped on the hood of her car.
That was a mistake.

He clung on thinking that she would stop.
How far could she drive with her husband hanging on to
    the hood?

A long way is the answer.
All the way to the interstate.
At speeds of up to seventy miles per hour.

After about twenty miles the police finally stopped her.

The man was fine.
They say with counseling and time he could resume a
   normal life.

Isn't it hilarious?
Why aren't you laughing?
Why are you looking at me like that?
Want to go for a drive?

Saying you grew up in Boston is not an excuse for your behavior

I know where you grew up.
I have met your family
and friends
and I am well aware of the fact that they are not normal.

But you are a grown man
with a family
and we don't live in Boston.

So you cannot scream at the television
during a hockey game and say
Fuck the Rangers!
I don't know what that means.
That's not a thing people say
even when children aren't in the room.

And do you really hope
that every member of

the New York Yankees
gets food poisoning?
Why would you say that?

Yes, Tom Brady is talented.
But I disagree that
he is a more important historical figure
than Gandhi.

Remind me again.
What's an *ahhs-hole*, anyway?

Where's that thing?

Where's that thing?
you ask me
looking in the cabinet above the stove.
The new one or old one, I reply,
fairly sure you know what I mean.
Old one.
Under the sink.
It's not there.
Just look.
I'm looking.
Look under that stuff.
It's not here.
The other stuff.
Nope.
Wait. You mean the green one?
No. Blue. I think it's blue.
Oh. That's in the drawer.
I checked the drawer.
Did you check behind the plastic thing?

We're talking about the same thing, right, the one with the weird top?

Of course.

Wait. Here it is.

Previously on *Useless Man*

Sometimes I think I could write a TV show.
I have ideas
that come to me all the time.

Here's one.

The pilot episode would take place in a home
as the children were getting ready for school.
We see the woman making lunches
helping with last-minute homework
tying shoes
packing backpacks
spooning cereal.
We see the man on the toilet on his iPad.

As the mother and children leave for school
the man tries to stand from the toilet.
But he's been sitting for so long
his legs have gone numb.
And he's stuck there all day.
Credits roll.

Please don't compare me to my mother

When you say that I am acting just like my mother
do you want me to go insane?
You must.
You know my mother is actually insane.
And that she drove the getaway car in a bank robbery
    once
with my older sister in the toddler seat in back
(she was not charged).
And once painted our house black to annoy my father.
And used a crossbow on squirrels in the yard because she
    felt they were "listening" to her.
And worried that former U.N. Secretary General Boutros
    Boutros-Ghali was following her.
So when I get angry that the car battery has died again
    and throw a hissy fit
please don't compare me to my mother.
Who is currently serving a five-year sentence for grand
    larceny.
Also I am a man.

To my fifth child

Of course I know your name.
It just helps me,
sometimes,
to say all of the others first
before I get to yours.
I know there aren't as many photos
of you as a baby
as there are of your older brothers and sisters.
And that yours is the only
Christmas stocking not handmade
and instead has your name
(which I know!)
written over the words "boy child."
And yes
we left you in the airport
in France that one time.
But that does *not* mean
we love you any less,
mister.

It just means we don't love you quite as much.

That came out wrong.

And yes, I said "mister"

because I couldn't think of your name right then.

Elegy

We are gathered here
in the upstairs bathroom
to honor the remarkably uninteresting life
of our pet Daryl.
You brought us a feeling akin to joy
during the eleven days we knew you.
If by "joy" you mean
an almost complete
lack of interest
in your existence
by our children
Iris and Ruby
from almost the moment
we arrived home from the pet store
after they begged me for you.
Also,
please forgive the many times
they whined that you weren't
a gerbil or a dog or giraffe.

And so
with this flush
we entrust you to the sea
via this toilet
in the company of a handful
of Goldfish crackers
compliments of Ruby.
Okay then.
No we are not getting a dog.
Yes you guys can watch *SpongeBob* now.

An attempt at a summation of a five-year-old's monologue

So let me see if I understand.
The tooth fairy makes no sense
because where would she keep the money?
And no one has ever seen a tooth fairy with a backpack
because how would a bag fit over her wings?
You can't with wings and you've tried.
Though it could be a tiny pouch that expanded to a giant
    pouch
but still she would have to fit so many kids' teeth
that it would be so heavy she would crash and maybe die.
Fair point.

And the Easter bunny can't be real
because how could he hold a basket
because no one has ever seen a rabbit's hands
because they don't have them.
Also, where would they get eggs and chocolate anyway
as chocolate is from Tokyo and rabbits aren't even allowed
    on planes.
Astrid in your class says so.

But Santa is real for several reasons.
First, you have seen his picture.
He can fly which is another thing.
And he can be thin and then later have a huge belly
and yet still fit in any standard chimney
as long as it's not on fire
which no one would do because who would want that
when you can get presents instead.

Makes perfect sense.

Letter back to a summer camper

Hi, sweetheart.
I am so sorry that you hate camp.
As well as your counselor,
the food,
your cabin mates,
and all the activities.
Camp Torture would be a better name.
But you only have seven more weeks.
And maybe it will stop raining at some point.
You're not missing anything fun at home.
Unless you think going to Paris
on a whim for five days is fun.
Which it was.
Also we go out to dinner almost every night.
And we're trying a new thing where your father and I
have coffee naked in the morning on the back deck.
Just because we can.
Oh. And we painted your bedroom.
And took down all that old artwork.

Which was not very good anyway (ha ha!).
And made it into an office.
That's not why you can't come home.
We want you to immerse yourself in nature
and experience life without screens.
And maybe go to boarding school come September.
It would be like summer camp for four years.
Won't that be fun?
Hang in there, sweetie.
We'll write from Spain.

Why?

I honestly don't know
the answer to almost anything you ask.
Why potato salad doesn't have lettuce in it.
Why the word "toilet" makes your friend Miles laugh.
Why the world is here.
I don't know anything.
I work in advertising.
What if I asked you "why" all day?
Why did you sit next to Kalyn at lunch today?
Why did Noah draw a bug with shoes on?
Why did you pretend our dog was a man called Dmitri
    who could read minds?
Why did you put peas in your nose at dinner?
Not so fun when the shoe's on the other foot is it?
Wait.
It is fun?
Why?

For Lulu & Hewitt

No offense to either of you
but I preferred the *idea*
of kids
to actual kids.

Who needs kids of their own
when you have nine nieces and nephews?
You get to be an uncle for a while.
Then you get to go home alone and sleep.

I blame your mother.
And her beautiful face.
And deeply kind spirit.
And her perfect answer
to why she wanted children.

Because I'm tired of worrying about myself.
I want to worry about someone else.

Can I tell you two a secret?

I was afraid.
I was afraid I wouldn't be good enough.
Too moody too needy too impatient too selfish too
    lacking.

But then you were born.
And you told me a secret.

Dad, you whispered.
All you have to do is
watch me and listen to me
and take my hand.
And I'll teach you how to be a father.

Then you spit up on my shirt.

Every night
before you go to sleep
I lean down and
whisper the same sentence.

In a lifetime of questions
and confusion
they are the truest words I know.

I am so lucky to be your dad.

ACKNOWLEDGMENTS

I would like to thank Kathy s., an Amazon.com reviewer of my previous book, *Love Poems for Married People*, who said, "This book is the worst." Also to the good people of the Russell Public Library, wherever that might be, who "HATED THIS BOOK SO MUCH" (their caps, not mine). They added, "It's crap." Thank you, Kathy and all of you at the Russell Public Library, for not believing in me. It was almost like being a kid again.

To Ivan Held, president of G. P. Putnam's Sons, who believed in *Love Poems for Married People* the moment it became a *New York Times* bestseller and who instantly green-lighted (-lit?) this book. As a result of the success of the first book, Ivan now lives in the South of France, where his paintings depict women with three boobs. (It's possible I'm thinking of Picasso in the 1920s and not Ivan.)

To Sally Kim, my editor, friend, sister-I-never-had, therapist, and guidance counselor.

To the team at G. P. Putnam's Sons. Ashley Hewlett (aka Kurt Andersen), Alexis Welby, Ashley McClay, Brennin Cummings, and Gabriella Mongelli.

To Susan Morrison and Emma Allen at *The New Yorker* for running the earliest of these poems in the first place.

Trusted readers and idea generators: Suzi Corcoran, Kim Gallagher, Dylan Blumstein, Lea Mastroberti, Alexa Englander, Rick Knief, Eric Carlson, Lex Carlson for swearing as a two-year-old, Linda Elriani, and Becky Gray.

To my children, Lulu and Hewitt.

And to my wife and best friend, Lissa. To whom I said, on our third date, "I don't think I want children." Thank God you ignored me.

ABOUT THE AUTHOR

John Kenney is the *New York Times* bestselling author of the poetry collection *Love Poems for Married People* and the novels *Talk to Me* and *Truth in Advertising*, which won the Thurber Prize for American Humor. He has worked for many years as a copywriter. He has also been a contributor to *The New Yorker* since 1999. He lives in Brooklyn, New York.